The ABCs of Self-Nurturing

Unlock Your Full Potential:
A Journal for Self-Discovery and Renewal

Laura Rochelle

Published by
WSA Publishing
333 E 14th Street
#3C
New York, NY 10003

Manufactured in the United States of America, or in the United Kingdom when distributed elsewhere.

AUTHOR Rochelle, Laura
TITLE *The ABCs of Self-Nurturing: Unlock Your Full Potential A Journal for Self-Discovery and Renewal.*
        ISBN: 978-1-961757-41-7
        eBook: 978-1-961757-42-4
        LCCN: 2024902219

Cover design by: Betsy Pippen
Copyediting by: Claudia Volkman
Interior design by: Betsy Pippen
Author photo by: Allan B. Sledge

WEBSITE: laurarochellecoach.com

Welcome to *The ABCs of Self-Nurturing Journal:*
Unlocking Your Full Potential on the Journey of Self-Discovery and Renewal

Beloved,

The fact that you are holding *The ABCs of Self-Nurturing Journal* in your hands is no accident. It's a moment of serendipity, a whispered message from the universe that you are ready to go on a remarkable journey. This isn't just a journal; it's an invitation—a loving invitation to immerse yourself in the profound art of self-discovery and nurturing.

You'll find more than just a collection of words and empty spaces within these pages. This is a thoughtfully crafted experience designed to plant the seeds of self-love, gently weed out negativity, and nourish your soul. It's a haven where you can reflect, heal, and grow.

Unlocking Your Full Potential with
The ABCs of Self-Nurturing

This journal is your companion, enriched with guided prompts and uplifting affirmations; it will be your steadfast partner in self-discovery. It's more than just paper and ink; it's a sanctuary where you can explore the depths of your heart, cultivate your inner garden, and transform your life.

A Holistic Roadmap for Self-Discovery and Renewal

Within these pages, you'll find reflective exercises and empowering affirmations corresponding to each letter of the alphabet. This holistic roadmap will guide you through the intricate path of self-discovery, offering insights and wisdom uniquely tailored to your needs.

This journal is a testament to your commitment to yourself. It's a declaration that you are ready to embrace the beauty of your existence and take the journey toward self-nurturing with *The ABCs of Self-Nurturing*. So, beloved, let these pages be your canvas, your sanctuary, and your confidant.

Are you ready to explore, grow, and transform? *The ABCs of Self-Nurturing Journal* is here to walk beside you every step of the way.

For additional resources that complement your journey, please visit my website at laurarochellecoach.com. Here, you'll find exclusive content, audio affirmations, and more to enhance your self-nurturing experience.

With love and gratitude,

Laura Rochelle

Prologue

In the following pages, *The ABCs of Self-Nurturing Journal* invites you to begin your journey of self-discovery and renewal. At its core lies a concept that will be your compass on this path to growth: Seeding, Weeding, and Feeding. So, let me introduce you to this concept. This is a concept I have found to be helpful in my and my clients' lives.

Seeding

Imagine your thoughts as seeds planted in the fertile soil of your mind. Are you nurturing positive seeds of self-love and confidence? Or have you unknowingly allowed harmful seeds of fear and self-doubt to take root? The seeds you cultivate today in your mind shape the life you'll harvest tomorrow.

Weeding

It's time to dig deep and remove the obstacles that no longer serve your growth. What must be uprooted from your life to let the brilliance of your existence shine through? Together, we'll identify and eliminate these hindrances.

Feeding

Consider how you're nourishing your heart and soul. What habits are you hungry for? How can you make space to nurture your inner self? Feeding your heart and soul with the right thoughts and actions will yield growth beyond your imagination.

Seeding, weeding, and feeding are the tools you'll use to explore the emotional, physical, and spiritual facets of your being. They are the keys to unlocking your full potential and building the life you desire.

In loving memory of my beloved grandmother, Eugenia Laura Bell Walker, better known as Laura B., and to my cherished mother, Joyce W. Johnson.

These two wonderful women have played the most pivotal roles in my life. My grandmother, the embodiment of unconditional love, showed me that I was enough, just as I am. My mother provided me with the space to embrace my true self, even when it felt unfamiliar to her, always encouraging me to give my best. Together, these two women formed a dynamic duo that guided me through life's twists and turns.

I am blessed to have had these loving women in my life. My mother continues to be a pillar of strength, and my dear grandmother, though no longer with us in body, remains a constant presence in my heart, reminding me time and again that my best is indeed good enough.

Abundant
Beloved
Contentment
Discovery
Enthusiasm
Fun
Grateful
Hope
Imagination
Joy
Kind
Love
Mindful
Nurture
Optimistic
Passion
Quest
Respect
Serenity
Thankful
Unique
Wonderful
X-Factor
Yearning
Zest

Abundant

over-sufficient; more than adequate, overflowing

A New Perspective:
Encourage Abundant Thinking

I embrace the power of abundant thinking. My attitude overflows with positivity and gratitude, reflecting the abundance that surrounds me. I am enough, and my life is sufficient in every way. When challenges arise, I embrace them as opportunities for growth and transformation. I release the familiar and welcome new, abundant thoughts that lead to life-changing possibilities. The leap into abundance thinking is a journey of self-discovery and empowerment. I take that leap confidently, knowing that abundance flows into every aspect of my life. I am the architect of my reality, and I choose to create a life filled with abundance and joy.

Cultivating an Abundant Mindset

Seeding Abundance

Start by sowing the seeds of abundance through visualization. Imagine your life filled with prosperity, joy, and fulfillment. Affirm daily that abundance is your birthright.

Weeding Out Limiting Beliefs

Identify and uproot any beliefs that limit your abundance. Replace scarcity thoughts with positive affirmations and empowering beliefs about your worthiness of abundance. If you think, *There's not enough to go around, so I must compete for and hoard resources,* you can say instead, "The universe is abundant, and there is more than enough for everyone."

Feeding Abundance with Gratitude

Nourish your soul with gratitude, for it is the sunshine that warms the garden of your beloved life. Write lovingly about the moments of self-love and blessings that grace your path. Celebrate the essence of your being with every heartfelt expression of thankfulness.

"Abundance is not something we acquire. It is something we tune into."

– Wayne Dyer

Seeding

How can I invite more abundance into my life today? When you think *There's not enough*, consider asking, "How can I make the most of what I have?" Start your day by acknowledging the wealth of opportunities around you.

_____

_____

_____

_____

_____

_____

_____

_____

_____

_____

Weeding

"Am I harboring a scarcity mindset?" If you find yourself worrying about what you don't have, try reframing it to focus on the abundance that already exists in your life.

_____

_____

_____

_____

_____

_____

Feeding

"How can I nurture a sense of abundance?" Consider dedicating time to express gratitude for what you have, or share your resources—be it time, skills, or material wealth—with others. Generosity often magnifies the feeling of abundance.

Beloved
greatly loved; dear to the heart

A New Perspective: Live a Beloved Life

Embrace self-love, for you are cherished and worthy. Journey within, discovering the depths of your heart. As you cherish yourself, the adventure of life blooms, allowing deeper connections with those beloved to you. You are dear to your own heart, and in that love, you find the key to living a beloved life with others. Embrace the adventure of self-discovery, for it leads to a life of abundance and joy. And let love guide your path, always, beloved. Remember, self-love is not selfish but a divine journey of honoring and treasuring the precious soul you are. Let the light of love guide your path always, beloved.

Cultivating a Beloved Life

Seeding Beloved Thoughts

Tenderly plant the seeds of self-love and acceptance in the garden of your heart. Visualize a life where love blooms abundantly, nourishing your soul with joy and compassion. Embrace the belief that you are worthy of the deepest affection and care.

Weeding Out Self-Doubt

Gently uproot any self-doubt or limiting beliefs that overshadow your worthiness. Replace them with empowering thoughts that honor your unique beauty and value. Uproot self-criticism and replace it with an affirmation like "I am deserving of love and embrace my flaws with kindness."

Feeding Your Heart with Gratitude

Nourish your soul with gratitude, for it is the sunshine that warms the garden of your beloved life. Write lovingly about the moments of self-love and blessings that grace your path. Celebrate the essence of your being with every heartfelt expression of thankfulness.

"A love story, at least a convincing one, requires three elements—the lover, the beloved, and the adventures they have together."
- Jane Smiley

Seeding

"How can I foster deeper connections and become a beloved individual?" If you think, *I am unworthy of love*, challenge it by saying, "I am inherently lovable and deserving of affection." Begin by acknowledging your innate worth and the love you already give and receive.

Weeding

"Am I holding on to patterns that keep me from love?" If you find yourself pushing people away or doubting their affection, consider reframing your thoughts. Replace fears of rejection with the willingness to be vulnerable and open.

Feeding

"How can I sustain and grow my status as a beloved individual?" Engage in acts of kindness and maintain meaningful conversations with the people who matter to you. Remember, love is a two-way street; it's as much about giving as it is about receiving.

Contentment
satisfied; in a state of peaceful happiness

A New Perspective: Be Content

In our fast-paced world, grant yourself rest and find satisfaction in the present moment. Practice the lost art of contentment by appreciating the good, no matter how small. Embrace the obstacles and challenges with a peaceful heart, knowing that your best efforts are enough. Because you are enough—because you are enough. Be kind to yourself and cultivate a state of inner peace and happiness. Let contentment be your guide to a fulfilled life, cherishing the simple joys and finding tranquility amidst life's demands. As you cultivate contentment, you create a peaceful and fulfilling life, rooted in self-kindness and gratitude. May this journey guide you to a state of peaceful happiness, where you appreciate the beauty of life's tapestry woven with contentment and inner peace.

Cultivating Contentment

Seeding Contentment

Start by sowing the seeds of contentment through mindfulness. Embrace the present moment and find joy in simple pleasures, nurturing a state of peaceful happiness.

Weeding Out Discontent

Identify and uproot any negative thoughts that hinder contentment. Replace them with positive affirmations and a focus on gratitude for what is already good in your life.

Feeding Contentment with Self-Kindness

Nourish your soul with self-compassion and acceptance. Embrace your imperfections and be satisfied with your efforts, knowing that you are enough.

"Be content with what you have; rejoice in the way things are. When you realize there is nothing lacking, the whole world belongs to you."

– Lao Tzu

Seeding

"How can I cultivate contentment today?" Consider practicing mindfulness or savoring simple pleasures to nurture peaceful happiness.

_____

_____

_____

_____

_____

_____

_____

_____

_____

_____

_____

Weeding

"What negative thoughts might be hindering my contentment?" When a thought like _I don't have enough_ surfaces, counter it by saying, "I am grateful for the abundance in my life."

_____

_____

_____

_____

_____

Feeding

"How can I bolster contentment with self-kindness?" Remind yourself of your worth or take a moment to celebrate your efforts, knowing you are enough.

Discovery

to get knowledge of, learn of, and get insight

A New Perspective: Encourage Discovery in Your Everyday Life

Cherish the adventure of self-discovery, for it holds the key to unlocking the beautiful essence of your true self. Take that brave first step inward, where knowledge and insight reside. Unwrap the unique gifts that belong to you and you alone. Your inner world is a sacred journey waiting to be explored, offering you positive possibilities beyond measure. So, in your everyday life, make room for the joy of discovery within. Allow self-discovery to illuminate your path, guiding you toward a life of fulfillment and purpose. It is there that you will find the real YOU, your ever-loving spirit, and the beauty of your everlasting soul.

Cultivating Discovery Within

Seeding Self-Exploration

Start by planting the seeds of self-discovery. Nurture curiosity and openness to learn more about your inner world.

Weeding Out Self-Doubt

Identify and uproot self-doubt and negative self-perceptions.
Replace them with self-compassion and positive affirmations
about your worthiness of self-discovery.

Feeding Your Inner Growth

Nourish your soul with self-reflection and mindfulness. Journal
about your discoveries, insights, and the beautiful uniqueness
that lies within you.

"The greatest discovery in life is self-discovery. Until
you find yourself, you will always be someone else."

- Myles Munroe

Seeding

"How can I initiate self-discovery today?" Consider sparking your curiosity or opening yourself up to new experiences and perspectives.

_____

_____

_____

_____

_____

_____

_____

_____

_____

_____

_____

Weeding

"What might be inhibiting my journey of discovery?" If you encounter thoughts like _I already know all there is to know about myself_, consider challenging them by saying, "There's always more to uncover and understand."

_____

_____

_____

_____

_____

_____

Feeding

"How can I nurture my process of discovery?" Perhaps dedicate time for reflective journaling or engage in activities that reveal more about your inner world and passions.

Enthusiasm

having a lively interest; absorbing or controlling
possession of the mind by any interest or pursuit

A New Perspective: Encourage and Share Enthusiasm

Embrace the childlike wonder within you, for enthusiasm is the spark that ignites the soul. Pursue your passions with a lively interest and eagerness, wearing enthusiasm like a crown of glory. Let curiosity lead you to new discoveries, for in enthusiasm, life's true magic unfolds. Embrace the zeal for living, and let it radiate from your being, inspiring others with its infectious joy. With enthusiasm as your guide, conquer challenges and savor each moment. Rekindle the flame of excitement, and let your heart dance with enthusiasm, for it is the key to a fulfilling and vibrant life. Cherish the crown of enthusiasm and wear it proudly.

Cultivating the Spark

Seeding Enthusiasm

Cultivate curiosity and spark new interests in your life. Embrace the childlike wonder within you and explore the world with fresh eyes and a lively spirit.

Weeding Out Negativity

Identify and uproot any thoughts or beliefs that dampen your enthusiasm. Replace self-doubt and negativity with affirmations that empower and inspire.

Feeding Enthusiasm with Joy

Nourish your soul with activities that bring joy and excitement. Engage in hobbies, adventures, and connections that fuel your passion and enthusiasm.

"Enthusiasm is the yeast that makes your hopes shine to the stars!"

- Henry Ford

Seeding

"How can I kindle enthusiasm today?" Think about reigniting an old interest or discovering a new hobby, allowing your innate curiosity to guide you.

_____
_____
_____
_____
_____
_____
_____
_____
_____
_____
_____

Weeding

"What might be dampening my enthusiasm?" If thoughts like *It's not worth the effort* emerge, consider countering these by telling yourself, "I embrace new experiences with an open heart."

_____
_____
_____
_____
_____
_____

Feeding

"How can I stoke the flames of my enthusiasm?" Partake in activities that have always brought you joy or explore new ones that might reignite passion and interest.

Fun

enjoyment, playfulness, amusement

A New Perspective: Have Fun as Much as You Can

Embrace the art of fun and let it weave its magic into the fabric of your life. Find laughter in everyday moments, nourishing your soul with joy and amusement. Don't let boredom's shadows linger; chase them away with your playfulness. Be the conductor of your own symphony of amusement. Dance like nobody's watching, laugh like it's your favorite song, and let happiness lead the way. Celebrate the ridiculous and wear a smile like a badge of honor. Giggle, grin, hoot, and holler—let your laughter echo through the corridors of your heart. Remember, you are the author of your own fun-filled story, so make it one that makes you laugh out loud!

Cultivating the Joyful Play

Seeding Fun

Plant the seeds of laughter and joy in your daily life. Embrace playfulness and seek out activities that bring a smile to your face.

Weeding Out Seriousness

Identify and uproot excessive seriousness that stifles fun. Replace rigidity with lightheartedness, freeing yourself to enjoy life's little pleasures.

Feeding Fun with Play

Nourish your soul with moments of play. Engage in activities that spark amusement and excitement, allowing fun to blossom and fill your days.

" Fun is good . "

- Dr. Seuss

Seeding

"How can I incorporate more fun into today?" Consider trying out a lighthearted activity or watching something that makes you laugh.

_____
_____
_____
_____
_____
_____
_____
_____
_____
_____
_____

Weeding

"What might be curbing my sense of fun?" If you find yourself thinking, *I don't have time for fun*, challenge this thought by saying, "I deserve moments of joy every day."

_____
_____
_____
_____
_____

Feeding

"How can I amplify the fun I experience?" Consider engaging in playful activities, games, or spontaneous adventures that ignite your sense of amusement.

Grateful

warmly appreciative of kindness or benefits received

A New Perspective: Be Grateful

Be grateful... Gratitude is the secret potion that transforms ordinary days into extraordinary ones. Embrace the power of thankfulness to illuminate your path, for even amidst the ups and downs, there's always something to cherish. Cultivate the art of counting blessings and relishing life's simplest joys. In gratitude, you'll find a sanctuary of peace and contentment. Let the warmth of appreciation infuse your heart and radiate through your soul. Look for the silver linings and focus on the good that surrounds you. Daily, let your heart's journal be filled with the gifts and kindness life offers. Be grateful, and you'll unlock a treasure trove of happiness and love that lasts a lifetime.

Cultivating a Grateful Heart

Seeding Gratitude

Start your day by planting seeds of gratitude. Awaken with the intention to appreciate the blessings that surround you. Speak words of thanks for the gift of life and the opportunities ahead.

Weeding Out Negativity

Identify and uproot any negative thoughts or complaints that overshadow gratitude. Replace them with positive affirmations and appreciation for the smallest joys. For example, replace complaints like "I hate Mondays" with "I appreciate the new week's possibilities." Transform "I can't do this" into "I am grateful for the chance to learn and grow."

Feeding Gratitude with Journaling

Nourish your soul with a gratitude journal. Write daily entries about the kindness and benefits you receive. Savor the goodness, and watch gratitude bloom and flourish in your heart.

"Gratitude turns what we have into enough, and more. It turns denial into acceptance, chaos into order, confusion into clarity...it makes sense of our past, brings peace for today, and creates a vision for tomorrow."

— Melody Beattie

Seeding

"How can I infuse more gratitude into my morning?" Think about beginning the day with a moment of thanks, perhaps listing three things you're grateful for right when you wake up.

_____
_____
_____
_____
_____
_____
_____
_____
_____
_____
_____

Weeding

"What negative thoughts might be obscuring my gratitude?" When you catch yourself thinking, *I hate Mondays*, consider reframing this as "I appreciate the new week's possibilities."

_____
_____
_____
_____
_____
_____
_____

Feeding

"How can I deepen my sense of gratitude daily?" Consider jotting down moments of kindness or blessings you've experienced, allowing the act of journaling to magnify your gratitude.

Hope

a feeling of expectation and desire for a
certain thing to happen

A New Perspective: Encourage Hope

Hope is the whisper of courage that resides within
my soul. Like a flame, it ignites my spirit and
lights the path ahead. With hope, I rise above life's
challenges, knowing that brighter days await. I feed
hope by seeking inspiration, surrounding myself with
positivity, and holding tightly to faith. Even in the
darkest moments, hope remains steadfast, guiding me
through uncertainty. Like a faithful companion, hope
accompanies me on this journey, reminding me that
possibilities are endless. Embracing hope, I dance
with dreams and embrace the beauty of what's to come
In hope, I find the strength to smile at the future,
knowing it holds promise and wonder.

Cultivating Hopeful Horizons

Seeding Hope

Plant seeds of hope in your heart and
mind, nurturing them with positive
affirmations and envisioning a future
filled with possibilities.

Weeding Out Despair

Identify and uproot negative thoughts that hinder hope. Replace them with empowering beliefs that fuel optimism and resilience. (For example, a Despairing thought: *Nothing ever goes my way.* Empowering belief: *Every challenge is an opportunity for growth.*)

Feeding Hope with Positivity

Nourish hope daily by seeking out positive influences, uplifting stories, and inspiring messages. Surround yourself with people who uplift and encourage you, and engage in activities that bring you joy and fulfillment. Embrace hope as a constant source of inspiration and motivation on your journey. Let hope be the guiding star that leads you towards your dreams and aspirations, and remember that with hope in your heart, anything is possible. Feed hope with love, gratitude, and the belief that the best is yet to come. Embrace hope as a powerful force that fuels your spirit and propels you towards a future filled with endless possibilities.

"Hope is the thing with feathers that perches in the soul and sings the tune without the words and never stops at all."

— Emily Dickinson

Seeding

"How can I cultivate hope today?" Affirm your aspirations and visualize a future brimming with opportunities.

_____

_____

_____

_____

_____

_____

_____

_____

_____

_____

_____

Weeding

"What thoughts might be diminishing my sense of hope?" When you feel like "Nothing ever goes my way," try reframing it as, "Every challenge is an opportunity for growth."

_____

_____

_____

_____

_____

_____

Feeding

"How can I reinforce hope daily?" Think about engaging with uplifting stories, surrounding yourself with positive individuals, or indulging in activities that rekindle joy and anticipation for the future.

Imagination
the process of producing ideal creations

A New Perspective:
Ignite Your Imagination

Encourage and ignite your imagination, for within its realm lies a wonderful experience of creating ideal possibilities. In the world of imagination, promising opportunities unfold, waiting to be explored. Dive deep into your thoughts and mind, for imagination opens doors and creates paths of endless potential. Visualize, talk out, and walk out the coming attractions of your life. You are the director, producer, and star of this creation. Your imagination paints the canvas of your future, whether that's a beautiful love story, a thrilling adventure, or a captivating drama. Embrace the power of imagination, and with every playful creation, pave the way to a wonderful life, bringing your dreams to life. Imagine that!

Cultivating Imaginative Realms

Seeding Imagination

Delve into the world of possibilities, visualize ideal creations, and explore promising opportunities that await your imagination.

Weeding Out Limiting Thoughts

Identify and uproot any beliefs that stifle your creative potential. Replace doubts and restrictions with affirmations that nurture imaginative thinking.

Feeding Imagination with Playfulness

Engage in playful exercises, visualize, and create vivid mental pictures of your dreams and aspirations. Embrace the role of the director, producer, and star of your life's story.

"Your imagination is everything. It is the preview of life's coming attractions."

- Albert Einstein

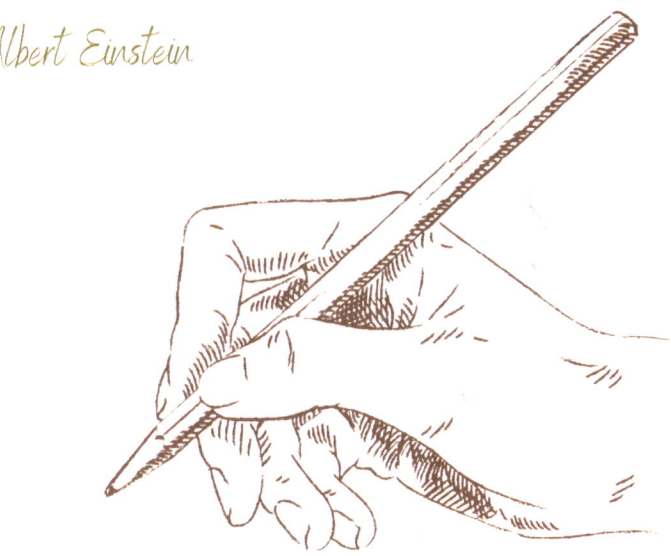

Seeding

"How can I spark my imagination today?" Consider visualizing your dream scenarios or brainstorming new, innovative ideas.

_____

_____

_____

_____

_____

_____

_____

_____

_____

_____

_____

_____

Weeding

"What might be inhibiting my imaginative flow?" If thoughts like *That's unrealistic* arise, try reframing by saying, "All great ideas started as dreams."

_____

_____

_____

_____

_____

_____

Feeding

"How can I nurture my imagination?" Think about doing creative exercises, doodling, or letting your mind wander without constraints, embracing the infinite possibilities.

Joy

the emotion of great delight or happiness caused by
something exceptionally good or satisfying

A New Perspective:
Live a Life of Joy

In every moment, I choose to live a life of joy, embracing the profound delight and happiness that comes from life's exceptional blessings. I find joy in the simple pleasures and the grand adventures, knowing that within each experience lies a source of profound satisfaction. I radiate joy from within, allowing it to uplift and inspire those around me. I see the beauty in every day and savor the goodness that surrounds me. With a heart full of gratitude, I am immersed in a life of joy, relishing the journey and finding happiness in all that is exceptionally good.

Cultivating a Joyful Heart

Seeding Joy

Plant the seeds of joy by choosing to focus on the positive aspects of your life. Embrace gratitude and mindfulness to cultivate a joyful perspective.

Weeding Out Negativity

Identify and uproot any thoughts or beliefs that hinder your ability to experience joy. Replace negativity with affirmations that promote happiness and delight.

Feeding Joy with Appreciation

Nourish your spirit with daily practices that bring you joy. Engage in activities that make your heart sing and create a sense of delight. Surround yourself with people and experiences that uplift your spirit.

" Joy is not in things; it is in us. "

- Richard Wagner

Seeding

"How can I sow joy in my day?" Consider cherishing positive moments or practicing gratitude for life's blessings.

_____

_____

_____

_____

_____

_____

_____

_____

_____

_____

_____

_____

Weeding

"What might be overshadowing my joy?" If you catch yourself thinking, _Today was a waste_, tell yourself instead, "Every day brings its own lessons and joys."

_____

_____

_____

_____

_____

_____

Feeding

"How can I enhance my daily joy?" Think about engaging in a cherished hobby or spending quality time with loved ones who lift your spirits.

Kind
considerate or helpful

A New Perspective: Choose to Be Kind

In the tapestry of life, I choose kindness as my thread, weaving a beautiful story of compassion and joy. I've felt the uplifting power of kindness, the way it envelops hearts in warmth, and leaves smiles on faces. Like a cozy blanket of compassion, it creates ripples of goodness that extend far beyond what I can see. Kindness doesn't cost a thing, but its impact is immeasurable.

So, I embrace the magic of kindness, spreading it generously, one small gesture at a time. With each act of consideration and every helping hand, I create a ripple effect of positivity that touches lives. I hold the power to make a difference, to bring light to the world and make it kinder, one act of compassion at a time. Let my heart be the source of kindness, and together, let us make our world a brighter, kinder, and more beautiful place.

Cultivating the Power of Kindness

Seeding Kindness

Plant the seeds of kindness by setting intentions to be considerate and helpful in your interactions. Choose to see the opportunities for kindness that surround you.

Weeding Out Negativity

Identify and uproot any thoughts or behaviors that hinder your ability to be kind. Replace judgment with understanding and criticism with compassion.

Feeding Kindness with Actions

Nourish your spirit by actively engaging in acts of kindness. Extend a helping hand, offer a word of encouragement, or simply lend a listening ear. Let your actions be guided by empathy and love.

"Be kind whenever possible. It is always possible."
- Dalai Lama

Seeding

"How can I integrate more kindness into my day?" Think about complimenting someone genuinely, offering assistance where you can, or simply acknowledging others with a smile.

_____

_____

_____

_____

_____

_____

_____

_____

_____

_____

_____

_____

Weeding

"What might be preventing my acts of kindness?" If you notice thoughts like *Why should I bother?* consider thinking instead, *Every act of kindness makes a difference.*

_____

_____

_____

_____

_____

Feeding

"How can I manifest kindness today?" Think about writing a note of appreciation, helping someone in need, or just being there for someone with a listening heart.

Love
warm attachment, enthusiasm, or devotion

A New Perspective: Encourage Love, Love and More Love

Encourage love, love, and more love. This four-letter word holds immense power, its warmth embraces us in every way. Love, which is not an everyday occurrence, evokes deep passion, tender affection, and lifelong connections. But here's the challenge: love yourself too. Embrace self-love, accepting yourself, flaws and all, with grace and kindness. Feel the emotional you, express true feelings respectfully, and find your voice. Connect with your powerful source within, the unconditional love that nourishes and empowers. Love speaks of forgiveness, encouragement, and self-awareness. Experience the love within, a journey not to be missed. Love yourself deeply—and watch how it transforms your world.

Cultivating the Blooms of Self-Love

Seeding Self-Love

Plant the seeds of self-love by acknowledging your worthiness and practicing self-compassion. Embrace your strengths and imperfections, and nurture the relationship you have with yourself.

Weeding Out Self-Criticism

Identify and uproot self-critical thoughts that hinder self-love. Replace them with affirmations of self-acceptance and positivity. Challenge the inner critic and choose self-kindness.

Feeding Self-Love with Nurturing Practices

Nourish your soul with self-care rituals that affirm your self-worth. Engage in activities that bring you joy, relaxation, and a sense of fulfillment. Prioritize your well-being and let self-love flourish.

"You yourself, as much as anybody
in the entire universe, deserve your love and affection."

– Buddha

Seeding

"What does love mean to me?" Reflect on the significance of love in your life, both in giving and receiving. If you find yourself thinking, *I'm not worthy of love,* tell yourself instead, "Everyone deserves love, including me."

_____
_____
_____
_____
_____
_____
_____
_____
_____
_____

Weeding

"Am I carrying any barriers to love?" Identify thoughts or past experiences that may be blocking you from experiencing love fully. When a thought like *Love always ends in pain*, enters your mind, challenge it by saying, "Love has the power to heal and uplift."

_____
_____
_____
_____
_____

Feeding

"How can I cultivate more love in my life?" Think about ways you can open yourself up to love. Whether it's through meaningful conversations, acts of kindness, or learning to love yourself, consider how you can enrich your life with more love.

Mindful
conscious or aware of something

A New Perspective: Be Mindful

In the present moment, I choose to be mindful—conscious and aware of every breath, every thought, and every emotion. With a calm and centered spirit, I embrace the richness of each experience. Mindfulness becomes my compass, guiding me through life's twists and turns with clarity and grace. I savor the beauty of the journey, fully immersed in the wonder of the now. In the art of mindfulness, I discover the power to respond with wisdom, to cultivate inner peace, and to connect deeply with myself and others. With each mindful step, I create a life of purpose, presence, and profound joy.

Cultivating Mindful Awareness

Seeding Mindfulness

Plant the seeds of mindfulness by grounding yourself in the present moment. Embrace your breath, sensations, and thoughts, cultivating a practice of conscious awareness.

Weeding Out Distractions

Identify and uproot the distractions that hinder mindfulness. Replace scattered thoughts with focused presence, gently guiding your attention back to the here and now.

Feeding Mindfulness with Practice

Nourish your soul with regular mindfulness practice. Engage in meditation, mindful breathing, and mindful activities to deepen your awareness and connection with the present moment.

"Be mindful. Be grateful. Be positive. Be true. Be kind."

— Roy T. Bennett

Seeding

"How can I foster mindfulness right now?" Consider taking a few deep breaths, feeling the air flow in and out and grounding yourself in the present.

_____
_____
_____
_____
_____
_____
_____
_____
_____
_____

Weeding

"What distractions might be pulling me away from this moment?" If you find your mind wandering to past events or future worries, gently redirect it back to the present, acknowledging the thought and letting it pass.

_____
_____
_____
_____
_____

abcdefghijklmnopqrstuvwxyz

Feeding
"How can I further deepen my mindfulness practice?" Think about
setting aside dedicated time for meditation or trying a mindful
activity, like a walking meditation or attentively drinking a cup
of tea.

Nurture
to care for and encourage the growth or
development of, cherish

A New Perspective: Nurture Yourself

Nurture yourself with gentleness, love, and
kindness. Embrace the beautiful blend of mind,
body, heart, and soul that makes you uniquely you.
Take time for self-care, affirming your heart with
loving words of positivity. Cherish
your body with rest, care, and nourishment for a
vibrant life. Expand the wonders of your mind,
embracing new knowledge and skills fearlessly.
Tune in to your soul's purpose, aligning with your
divine path. This journey of self-nurturing is not
selfish but an everlasting love, a healthy dose of
self-love. Endorse the satisfaction guaranteed only
by you. Remember, you are worthy of love and care,
and nurturing yourself is a beautiful
act of self-preservation.

Cultivating Self-Nurturing

Seeding Self-Nurturing

Begin by planting the seeds of self-
nurturing in your daily life. Make
a commitment to prioritize self-care,
self-love, and self-compassion.

d out
alth
ial v
n I
ne of
somet
lackth
lay.
watch tic
night
ating,
or all i
g-place
f big-c
me yea
nich I
berwe

Weeding Out Neglect

Identify and uproot any habits or beliefs that neglect self-nurturing. Replace self-criticism with self-kindness, and let go of any actions that undermine your well-being.

Feeding Self-Nurturing with Rituals

Nourish your soul with nurturing rituals. Create a daily self-care routine that includes activities that replenish your energy, bring you joy, and connect you with your inner self.

"Nurture yourself — life without it is just existing."
- Laura Rochelle

Seeding

"How do I set aside some time just for myself?" Set the intention to make the time, even if it's a few minutes of quiet reflection or a short walk.

_____
_____
_____
_____
_____
_____
_____
_____
_____
_____

Weeding

"What habits might be preventing my self-nurturing?" If you notice tendencies to push yourself too hard or brush aside your own needs, choose to pivot toward self-kindness and understanding.

_____
_____
_____
_____
_____

Feeding

"How can I nourish my self-nurturing rituals?" Think about integrating a cherished self-care activity into your day, such as a calming skincare routine or a moment of gratitude journaling.

Optimistic
hopeful and confident about the future

A New Perspective: Be Optimistic

I embrace an optimistic mindset, radiating hope and confidence about the future. I choose to see the bright side of every situation and believe in the possibilities that lie ahead. With optimism as my guide, I overcome challenges with resilience and grace. I attract positivity and abundance into my life, creating a fulfilling and joyful journey. I trust in my own abilities and in the goodness of the universe. Today, and every day, I choose optimism and embrace a future filled with endless possibilities.

Cultivating Optimism

Seeding Optimism

Plant the seeds of optimism by shifting your focus towards positive outcomes. Visualize your goals and dreams as achievable, and cultivate an attitude of hope for the future.

d out
alth
ial y
n I
ne of
somet
lackth
ay.
watch tic
night
ating,
or all i
g-place
f big-c
me yea
ich I
berwe

Weeding Out Negativity

Identify and uproot negative thoughts that hinder optimism. Replace self-doubt and pessimism with empowering beliefs that foster confidence and trust in your journey.

Feeding Optimism with Affirmations

Nourish your soul with daily affirmations that reinforce your optimistic mindset. Speak words of encouragement and positivity to yourself, fostering a sense of hope and confidence in your capabilities.

"Optimism is the faith that leads to achievement. Nothing can be done without hope and confidence."
— Helen Keller

Seeding

"How can I sow optimism today?" Ponder on moments where you overcame challenges in the past and trust that positive outcomes lie ahead.

_____

_____

_____

_____

_____

_____

_____

_____

_____

_____

_____

Weeding

"What negative thoughts might be clouding my optimism?" If you catch yourself thinking, _This won't work_, reframe it by telling yourself, "I'll do my best and learn from the outcome."

_____

_____

_____

_____

_____

_____

Feeding
"How can I strengthen my optimism?" Consider adopting a daily affirmation, like "I am capable and open to life's abundant possibilities," to fuel your hopeful perspective.

Passion
an intense desire or enthusiasm for something

A New Perspective: Live with Passion

I embrace life with passion, for it infuses each day with vibrant purpose and boundless joy. A life lived with passion is anything but boring; it is a magnificent journey of discovery and fulfillment. I follow my heart's desires and pursue my dreams fearlessly, knowing that within this intense desire lies the key to unlock my true potential. With every step, I radiate the energy of passion, inspiring others to live boldly and embrace the beauty of their own unique journey. In the pursuit of my passions, I find the essence of a life truly lived.

Cultivating Passion

Seeding Passion

Plant the seeds of passion by exploring your interests and uncovering what excites your soul. Allow curiosity to guide you towards activities that ignite your enthusiasm.

Weeding Out Stagnation

Identify and uproot any habits or thoughts that hinder your passion. Release any fear or doubt that holds you back from pursuing what truly sets your heart on fire.

Feeding Passion with Action

Fuel your passion through action. Maintain commitment and persistence as you stride toward your dreams, whether they're big or small. Every step you take ignites the flames of your enthusiasm, propelling you into a life drenched in purpose and joy.

"Follow your passion. It will lead you to your purpose."

– Oprah Winfrey

Seeding

"What excites me?" Reflect on the interests or activities that stir your enthusiasm. If a thought like *I'm not passionate about anything* crosses your mind, counter it by saying, "I have the potential to discover what ignites my soul."

_____

_____

_____

_____

_____

_____

_____

_____

_____

_____

_____

Weeding

"Are there any obstacles dulling my passion?" Identify fears, doubts, or other barriers that could be inhibiting your passionate pursuits. If you catch yourself thinking, *I could never do that,* rephrase this and say, "What's the first small step I could take?"

_____

_____

_____

_____

Feeding

"How can I fuel my passion today?" Consider actionable steps to engage with what excites you. Whether it's setting aside time to dive into a hobby or researching opportunities related to your passion, think about how you can actively foster your enthusiasm.

Quest

a search for something, to seek out

A New Perspective: What Is Your Quest?

In the pursuit of self-discovery, I embark on a quest of purpose and understanding. As I journey forward, I seek the treasures of wisdom and inner truth. My quest leads me to explore the depths of my soul, searching for meaning in every step I take. Sometimes the path may diverge sideways, or ascend upwards, while at other times, it may descend into moments of reflection. Yet, through every twist and turn, I remain steadfast in my quest, for within this exploration lies the essence of a life fully lived.

Cultivating the Journey of Self-Discovery

Seeding Self-Discovery

Plant the seeds of curiosity and intention as you embark on a quest of purpose and self-understanding. Embrace the desire to uncover the hidden treasures within your own being and the world around you.

Weeding Out Doubt

Identify and uproot the weeds of self-doubt and hesitation that may hinder your journey of self-discovery. Replace them with self-affirmations and the unwavering belief in your ability to uncover the truths you seek.

Feeding the Quest

Nourish your soul with the fuel of exploration and reflection. Engage in activities that encourage introspection and growth, whether through journaling, meditation, or engaging in conversations with mentors and fellow seekers. Every step forward feeds the flames of your self-discovery journey, leading you closer to the essence of your true self.

"He who completes a quest does
not merely find something.
He becomes something."
    - Lev Grossman

Seeding

"How can I honor my personal quest today?" Consider setting intentions that align with your search for purpose or understanding. When you find yourself asking, "What's next?" consider instead, "What step can bring me closer to my quest?"

_____

_____

_____

_____

_____

_____

_____

_____

_____

_____

Weeding

"Am I ignoring or avoiding aspects of my quest?" If thoughts like *I'm not capable* or *It's too hard* arise, reframe them by saying, "This is an opportunity for growth."

_____

_____

_____

_____

_____

_____

Feeding

"How can I enrich my journey?" Whether it's delving into relevant literature, seeking guidance from mentors, or taking time for introspection, find ways to nurture the quest you're on.

Respect
to admire (someone or something) deeply, as a result of their abilities, qualities, or achievements

A New Perspective:
Respect Yourself and Others!

With a heart full of admiration and empathy, I choose to respect myself and others deeply. Embracing the uniqueness of each individual, I honor their abilities, qualities, and achievements. In this journey of compassion, I treat others with kindness, valuing their perspectives and experiences. Moreover, I extend the same reverence to myself, acknowledging my worth and celebrating my growth. In every interaction, I radiate respect, creating a space where understanding and harmony flourish. As I uplift and honor both myself and others, I foster a world filled with empathy, acceptance, and authentic connections.

Cultivating Empathy and
Authentic Connections

Seeding Respect

Begin by sowing the seeds of respect within your heart. Acknowledge your own worth and honor the unique qualities of others. Cultivate empathy as you recognize the diverse perspectives that enrich our human experience.

Weeding Out Disrespect

Identify and uproot any thoughts or behaviors that contribute to disrespect. Challenge stereotypes, judgments, and biases that hinder genuine admiration for others. Replace negative attitudes with open-mindedness and a willingness to understand.

Feeding Respect with Empathy

Nourish your soul with acts of kindness and empathy towards yourself and others. Practice active listening, engage in meaningful conversations, and seek to understand different viewpoints. Let your actions and words reflect the deep respect you hold for the abilities, qualities, and achievements of each individual.

"Respect for ourselves guides our morals, respect for others guides our manners."
— Laurence Sterne

Seeding

"How can I show respect to myself and others today?" Start by acknowledging your achievements, however small, and recognizing the value others bring into interactions. Celebrate differences and see them as strengths.

_____

_____

_____

_____

_____

_____

_____

_____

_____

_____

_____

Weeding

"Am I holding on to any biases or judgments?" When you catch yourself thinking, *They're just not like me*, tell yourself instead, "I wonder what I can learn from their perspective?"

_____

_____

_____

_____

_____

Feeding
"How can I deepen my understanding and respect for others?" Dive into multicultural books, attend workshops, or simply ask someone about their experiences. Listening without judgment is a powerful way to foster respect.

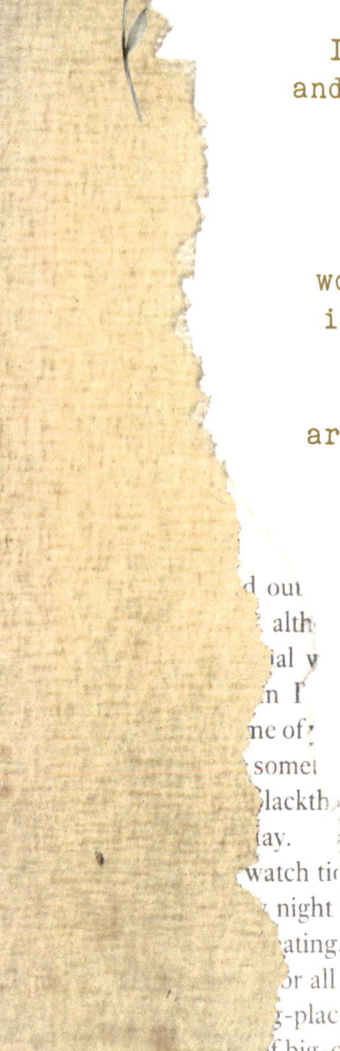

Serenity
the state of being calm and peaceful

A New Perspective:
Slow Down! Serenity Is Needed!

In the gentle embrace of serenity, I find tranquility and peace. I choose to slow down and savor each moment, for serenity does not rush, nor does it demand. It whispers softly, inviting me to rest and be present. In the stillness, I discover a profound calm that nurtures my soul. Serenity allows me to release worries and embrace the beauty of simplicity. Today, I invite serenity into my life, to dwell in its soothing presence and to find solace in its gentle rhythm. With each breath, I embrace the serenity within and around me, knowing that within its quiet grace, I find profound contentment.

Cultivating the Calm: Embracing Serenity in a Fast-Paced World

Seeding Serenity

Begin by acknowledging the need for serenity in your life. Recognize the value of calmness and peacefulness amidst the busyness of the world. Plant the intention to slow down and invite serenity into your daily experiences.

Weeding Out Chaos

Identify the factors that disrupt your sense of serenity. Weed out unnecessary commitments, distractions, and sources of stress. Create space for stillness and calm by letting go of what no longer serves your well-being.

Feeding Serenity with Presence

Nourish your soul with moments of presence and mindfulness. Embrace practices such as meditation, deep breathing, or simply observing the beauty around you. Feed your serenity by prioritizing moments of quiet reflection and inner peace.

"Serenity is not just an escape, but a precursor for acceptance, courage, wisdom and change."
   - Bill Crawford

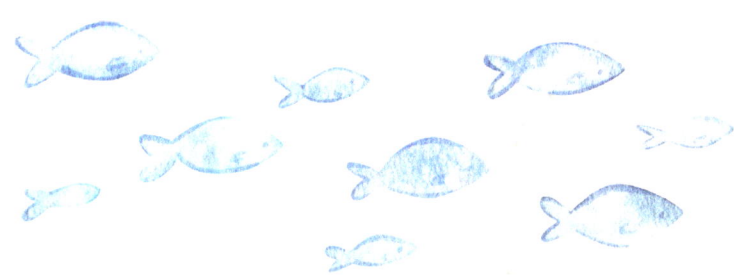

Seeding

"What steps can I take to cultivate serenity today?" Acknowledge the need for peace in your life. When the world feels overwhelming, remind yourself, "I can find peace within me," and seek out moments of stillness.

_____

_____

_____

_____

_____

_____

_____

_____

_____

Weeding

"Are there sources of chaos I can address?" When feeling frazzled, replace thoughts like *I can't handle this* with *I'll tackle one thing at a time.* Consider decluttering both physical spaces and mental commitments to create a serene environment.

_____

_____

_____

_____

Feeding

"How can I maintain a serene mind amidst daily challenges?" Adopt daily rituals such as a five-minute morning meditation. Taking a peaceful walk in nature or listening to calming music can help you nurture an inner landscape of serenity.

Thankful
conscious of benefit received

A New Perspective: Be Thankful— It Makes Life Work Better!

With a heart filled with gratitude, I choose to be thankful for life's blessings and benefits. Embracing thankfulness, life works better in magical ways. Each day, I acknowledge the gifts that enrich my journey, big and small. Conscious appreciation fosters a positive outlook, fueling my actions and interactions. Thankfulness transforms challenges into opportunities and moments into cherished memories. Embracing gratitude, I invite joy and harmony, creating a harmonious symphony that orchestrates the rhythm of my life.

Cultivating the Transforming Power of Thankfulness

Seeding Thankfulness

Begin by planting the seeds of thankfulness in your daily routine. Awaken with the intention to consciously appreciate the benefits and blessings that surround you. Plant the seeds of gratitude by acknowledging even the smallest gifts in your life.

Weeding Out Negativity

Identify and uproot negative thoughts that hinder your ability to be thankful. Replace complaints and dissatisfaction with positive affirmations and a focus on the benefits you've received.

Feeding Thankfulness with Reflection

Nourish your spirit by taking time to reflect on the things you're thankful for. Keep a gratitude journal to jot down daily moments of appreciation. Feed your thankfulness by pausing throughout the day to express gratitude for the positive experiences that come your way.

"Be thankful for what you have; you'll end up having more. If you concentrate on what you don't have, you will never, ever have enough."
– Oprah Winfrey

Seeding

"How can I cultivate thankfulness today?" Take a moment to identify small joys and victories, like a moment of laughter or a completed task. When you find yourself thinking, *I don't have enough,* ask yourself the question, "What do I already have that I can appreciate?"

_____

_____

_____

_____

_____

_____

_____

_____

_____

_____

Weeding

"Are there thoughts or attitudes blocking my sense of gratitude?" If you catch yourself focusing on lack or complaining, try to reframe it by saying, "What's another way to see this situation?"

_____

_____

_____

_____

_____

Feeding

How can I deepen my sense of thankfulness?" Reflect on your blessings, perhaps by discussing them with a friend, or jotting them down during a quiet moment. These acts can help reinforce your sense of gratitude.

Unique

being without a like or equal, being the only one

A New Perspective: It's OK to Be Unique—It's What Makes You Special!

Embracing my uniqueness, I celebrate the gift of being one-of-a-kind. It's okay to be unique; it's what makes me special. I stand confidently in my individuality, knowing that there is no one else like me. With each step, I honor my authentic self, expressing my true essence without reservation. Embracing my distinct qualities and perspectives, I bring a valuable contribution to the world. I cherish the qualities that set me apart and use them as a canvas to paint a life that is authentically mine. It's okay to be unique, for in my uniqueness lies my strength and beauty.

Cultivating Your Authentic Uniqueness

Seeding Uniqueness

Begin by planting the seeds of self-acceptance and embracing your individuality. Recognize the qualities that make you unique and valuable. Seed your confidence by affirming that your uniqueness is what sets you apart in a beautiful way.

Weeding Out Comparison

Identify and uproot any tendencies to compare yourself with others. Replace self-doubt and insecurity with affirmations that highlight your individual strengths and attributes.

Feeding Uniqueness with Self-Love

Nourish your self-esteem by practicing self-love and self-care. Engage in activities that celebrate your unique qualities and talents. Feed your confidence by reminding yourself daily that your uniqueness is a gift to be cherished.

"To be yourself in a world that is constantly trying to make you something else is the greatest accomplishment."
- Ralph Waldo Emerson

Seeding

"What makes me unique?" Consider the qualities or experiences that set you apart. If you find yourself thinking, *I'm just like everyone else*, counter it by telling yourself, "I have my own unique blend of talents and perspectives."

_____
_____
_____
_____
_____
_____
_____
_____
_____
_____
_____

Weeding

"Am I comparing myself to others?" Recognize moments when you're measuring your worth based on someone else's accomplishments or traits. Turn thoughts like *I wish I were like them* into *What can I learn from them while still honoring my individuality?*

_____
_____
_____
_____
_____

Feeding

"How can I celebrate my uniqueness?" Think of ways to accentuate what makes you special. Whether that's indulging in activities that showcase your talents or surrounding yourself with people who appreciate your uniqueness, consider how you can continually affirm your individuality.

Value

relative worth, or importance; something
intrinsically desirable

A New Perspective: You Have Value—Yes You Do!

In the depths of your being, remember this truth: You have value—yes, you do! Within you lies a unique essence of worth and importance. Embrace the qualities that make you intrinsically valuable and desirable. Your presence in this world is a treasure, a contribution of immeasurable significance. In every moment, let this affirmation guide you to recognize your worthiness and to honor the core of who you are. Your journey is a testament to your inherent value, a beacon of light that radiates through the world. You have value, and that value brightens the lives of those around you.

Cultivating Your Inherent Worth

Seeding Your Inherent Value

Begin by planting the seeds of self-awareness and recognizing your intrinsic worth. Affirm that your value is not dependent on external factors, but is an inherent part of your being.

Weeding Out Self-Doubt

Identify and uproot any thoughts of self-doubt or feelings of inadequacy. Replace them with affirmations that remind you of your unique qualities and the importance you hold in the world.

Feeding Your Self-Worth with Self-Care

Nourish your self-worth through self-care and self-compassion. Engage in activities that uplift your spirit and remind you of your value. Feed your confidence by treating yourself with kindness and respect.

"You are valuable because you exist. Not because of what you do or what you have done, but simply because you are."
— Max Lucado

Seeding

"How can I recognize my own value today?" Contemplate your innate worth that goes beyond material or external validations. If a thought like *I'm not good enough* surfaces, counter it by saying, "I have inherent value that's not defined by external factors."

_____

_____

_____

_____

_____

_____

_____

_____

_____

Weeding

"Am I doubting my worth?" Catch instances when you belittle yourself or consider yourself inferior to others. Replace such thoughts with affirmations that reaffirm your value, such as "I bring something unique to the table."

_____

_____

_____

_____

_____

_____

Feeding

"How can I nourish my sense of self-worth?" Look for opportunities to reinforce your value. This could be through self-care rituals, engaging in work that fulfills you, or spending time with those who appreciate your worth. Explore ways to consistently acknowledge your value, inside and out.

Wonderful

exciting wonder, unusually good

A New Perspective: Feel Wonderful, Because You Are!

Feel wonderful, for you are a magnificent creation of exciting wonder, uniquely and unusually good. Embrace the beauty of your essence, for within you is a spark of brilliance that shines brightly. Each day, let this knowledge guide you, igniting your soul with joy and gratitude. Celebrate your individuality, knowing that you possess the power to create magic in your life and the lives of others. Embrace your worth, your potential, and your inner strength. You are a wonder to behold, and in your presence, the world becomes a more extraordinary place. Trust in the magic that lies within you, for you are a wonder to be celebrated.

Cultivating Your Inner Radiance

Seeding a Sense of Wonder

Plant the seeds of self-appreciation and wonder within yourself. Embrace your uniqueness and the exciting qualities that make you unusually good.

Weeding Out Self-Doubt

Identify and uproot any self-doubt or negative self-perceptions that hinder your ability to feel wonderful. Replace them with positive affirmations that reinforce your worth and brilliance.

Feeding Your Inner Radiance

Nourish your sense of wonder through self-care and self-love. Engage in activities that make you feel alive and excited. Feed your inner radiance with positive experiences and interactions.

"The most wonderful and amazing people are those, who are true to themselves."
– Anamika Mishra

Seeding

"How can I cultivate a sense of wonder in my life today?" Ponder the elements in your world that inspire awe. If you catch yourself taking life's miracles for granted, remind yourself, "There is wonder all around me."

_____

_____

_____

_____

_____

_____

_____

_____

Weeding

"Do I have any cynicism that's blocking my sense of wonder?" When you find yourself feeling jaded or too adult to enjoy life's simple joys, challenge that notion with thoughts like *Wonder is accessible at any age.*

_____

_____

_____

_____

_____

_____

_____

Feeding

"How can I nourish my sense of wonder?" Consider engaging in activities that spark your imagination and curiosity. This could be stargazing, exploring a new area, or simply observing the intricacies of a flower. Take time to appreciate the wonderful things around you and let that fuel your sense of awe.

X-Factor

a circumstance, quality, or person that has a strong but
unpredictable influence

A New Perspective: Express Your X-Factor— You Know You Have What It Takes!

Embrace your uniqueness and express your X-factor confidently, for you hold within you a powerful and unpredictable influence. You know you have what it takes to leave an indelible mark on the world. Embrace your extraordinary qualities and let them shine brightly. Your essence is unlike any other, and it is meant to be shared with the world. Embrace the beauty of your X-factor, for it is the key to unlocking your true potential. With every step, you leave a trail of inspiration, reminding others of the extraordinary influence they can have too. Express your X-factor fearlessly, and watch as you leave a lasting impact on the world around you.

Cultivating Your X-Factor: Unleash the Unpredictable Influence Within

Seeding Your X-Factor

Plant the seeds of self-confidence and uniqueness within yourself. Embrace your extraordinary qualities and recognize the powerful and unpredictable influence you hold.

Weeding Out Self-Doubt

Identify and uproot any self-doubt or thoughts that downplay your X-factor. Replace them with affirmations that empower and encourage you to express your unique qualities.

Feeding Your Unique Essence

Nourish your X-factor by taking bold actions that showcase your uniqueness. Step out of your comfort zone and share your talents and qualities with the world. Feed your unique essence by surrounding yourself with positive influences and opportunities for growth.

"Your X-factor is what makes you unique.
Embrace it, express it, and don't be afraid to let it shine."
                            - Anonymous

Seeding

"What makes me unique?" Imagine embracing your quirks and idiosyncrasies as your own special X-factor.

_____
_____
_____
_____
_____
_____
_____
_____
_____
_____

Weeding

"Are there self-limiting thoughts hindering the full expression of my X-factor?" What if the things considered flaws were actually unique attributes?

_____
_____
_____
_____
_____
_____
_____

Feeding

"How could I amplify what makes me unique?" Exploring creative outlets or new experiences could be ways to further understand and express this X-factor.

Yearning

a feeling of intense longing for something,
a tender or urgent longing

A New Perspective: Encourage a Yearning for Lifelong Learning!

With an open heart and curious mind, I encourage a yearning for lifelong learning. Yearning for knowledge, I embrace each opportunity to grow and expand my understanding of the world. I seek wisdom in every experience, both big and small. Learning becomes a joyful journey of discovery, enriching my life with new perspectives and insights. I cherish the joy of discovery and the growth it brings. In the pursuit of knowledge, I am forever a student of life, open to the lessons it presents. With each step forward, I nurture my yearning for lifelong learning, enriching my journey and empowering my soul.

Cultivating the Yearning for Lifelong Learning

Seeding a Yearning for Lifelong Learning

Plant the seeds of curiosity and excitement for lifelong learning within your heart and mind. Embrace the idea that every experience is an opportunity to gain new knowledge and insights.

Weeding Out Limiting Beliefs

Identify and uproot any limiting beliefs that hinder your yearning for learning. Replace them with affirmations that encourage a growth mindset and a hunger for knowledge.

Feeding Your Curiosity

Nourish your yearning for lifelong learning by actively seeking out new experiences, challenges, and opportunities to expand your knowledge. Engage in activities that ignite your curiosity and stimulate your desire to learn.

"Lifelong learning ignites the fire of knowledge within, sparking a journey of continual growth and exploration."
– Laura Rochelle

Seeding

"What if each experience was seen as a lesson waiting to be uncovered?" Cultivating a mindset open to learning can be enriching.

_____

_____

_____

_____

_____

_____

_____

_____

_____

_____

Weeding

"What thoughts might be standing in the way of a thirst for knowledge?" Reframe the challenges as opportunities and see how the narrative changes.

_____

_____

_____

_____

_____

_____

Feeding

"What might a deeper dive into unfamiliar topics or skills look like?" Engaging with new material or communities could be potential avenues for feeding this curiosity.

Zest

an enjoyably exciting quality, keen enjoyment

A New Perspective: Live Life with Zest—Don't Waste It!

I celebrate life's vibrant essence, savoring its precious moments with unwavering joy. Each day is a gift meant to be embraced, not wasted in the shadows. I dance with enthusiasm, my heart singing with delight. In every action, I infuse an enjoyably exciting quality, igniting my soul with passion. Challenges are stepping stones to growth, setbacks valuable lessons. Surrounded by uplifting souls, I cherish laughter and relish simple pleasures. With unwavering commitment, I paint my life's canvas with vibrant colors, authentically living each extraordinary moment. I am the artist of my journey, and I embrace life with zest.

Cultivating a Zestful, Vibrant Life

Seeding a Zestful Approach to Life

Plant the seeds of enthusiasm and excitement for life within your heart. Embrace each day as a gift and an opportunity to experience joy and passion.

Weeding Out Negativity

Identify and uproot any negative thoughts or habits that hinder your zest for life. Replace them with positive affirmations and a focus on the things that bring you joy and excitement.

Feeding Your Enthusiasm

Nourish your zest for life by engaging in activities that bring you keen enjoyment and excitement. Surround yourself with people and experiences that uplift your spirits and ignite your passion.

"If you have zest and enthusiasm, you attract zest and enthusiasm. Life does give back in kind."
—Norman Vincent Peale

Seeding

"What brings me joy and energy?" Imagine beginning each day with an intention to seek out what enlivens you.

_____

_____

_____

_____

_____

_____

_____

_____

_____

_____

Weeding

"Do negative thoughts sap my zest for life?" Instead of saying, "I have to," tell yourself, "I get to." See everyday tasks as opportunities for enthusiasm.

_____

_____

_____

_____

_____

_____

_____

Feeding

"How could I cultivate more zest in my daily life?" Being around uplifting people or engaging in joyful activities can be a source of renewed energy and enthusiasm.